I0814211

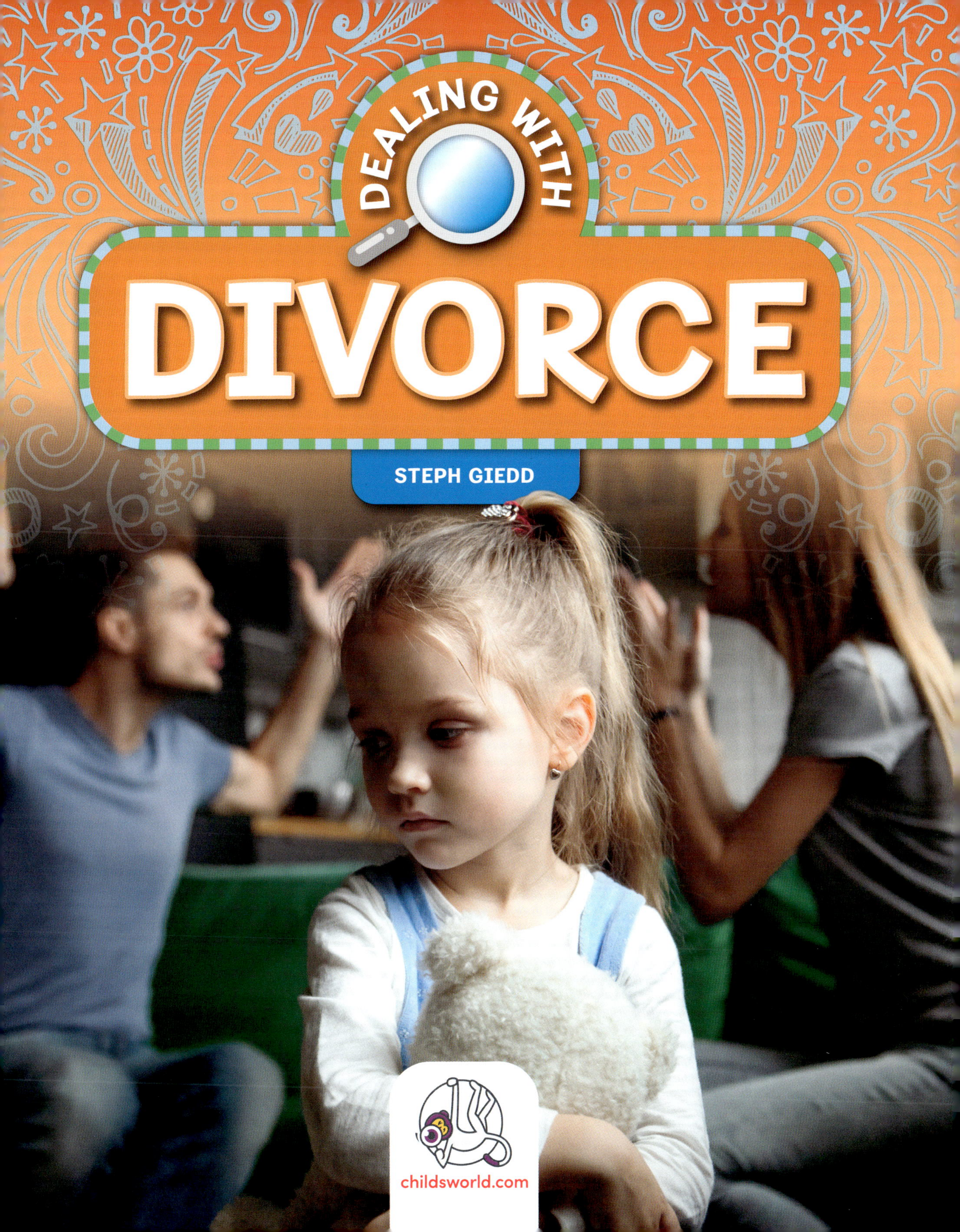
DEALING WITH
DIVORCE
STEPH GIEDD
childsworld.com

Published by The Child's World®
800-599-READ · www.childsworld.com

Photography Credits
Photographs ©: Shutterstock Images, cover, 1, 7 (top right), 8, 11, 15, 18; iStockphoto, 5, 7 (bottom left), 22; Monkey Business Images/Shutterstock Images, 7 (top left); Soloviova Liudmyla/Shutterstock Images, 7 (bottom right); Dragon Images/Shutterstock Images, 12–13; Drazen Zigic/Shutterstock Images, 17; Bongkarn Graphic/Shutterstock Images, 20

ISBN Information
9781503885356 (Reinforced Library Binding)
9781503885585 (Portable Document Format)
9781503886223 (Online Multi-user eBook)
9781503886865 (Electronic Publication)

LCCN 2023937461

Printed in the United States of America

Steph Giedd is a former high school English teacher who now works as an editor. Originally from southern Iowa, Giedd lives in Minneapolis, Minnesota, with her husband, daughter, and pets.

TABLE OF CONTENTS

When Divorce Happens

Sometimes families go through a big change called divorce. A divorce is when two people end their marriage. Parents often think carefully before they make this life-changing decision. There are many reasons parents might decide to get a divorce. It can result in a lot of changes in the family. But divorce does not mean that a family is broken. It does not mean that parents do not love their children.

One parent might move out of the home after a divorce.

Families often change after a divorce. Children might start living with just one parent. They might move between two homes. If a parent gets remarried, stepparents and stepsiblings might join the family. Change can be scary. But all families are unique. No one kind of family is better than another.

Family Structures

Some children live with both of their parents.

Some children live with one parent.

Some children live with stepparents and stepsiblings.

Sometimes children move back and forth between two homes.

All families look different. After a divorce, a family might change.

A person might feel sad or anxious if his parents fight. He should walk away from the situation. It is not his job to end or fix the fight.

A divorce can cause strong emotions. Kids may feel uncertain and **anxious**. They may have questions, such as who they will live with. They may also feel sad or angry that their family is changing. Kids might feel a sense of loss, especially if they will now see one parent less often. Sometimes kids may feel **guilty**. They might think that their parents' divorce is their fault. But that is not the case.

Everyone deals with divorce differently. Whatever emotions a child may feel during this challenging time are OK. There are many ways to handle those feelings and start to feel better.

Coping with Divorce

Going through a divorce is tough for everyone involved. But there are ways to **cope**. It is important for kids to continue caring for themselves. Eating healthy meals and getting enough sleep both help people feel good. Doing something fun can help people feel better, too. This is true even during hard times. Practicing calming exercises can also be helpful. People could go for a walk or take deep breaths.

A person might find joy with a parent or other relative, such as a grandparent. This is one way she might take care of herself.

Doing homework is one example of a daily routine. It is important to keep up healthy routines, even during big life changes.

Having **routines** helps things feel more normal. It can help to keep up old routines when possible. For example, people can go to bed at the same time every night. Sometimes divorce causes routines to change. Children might have a new schedule for moving between two homes. A parent might have new rules. It is important to **adapt** to new routines.

Kids go through a lot of emotions during a divorce. It is important to share those emotions. That way, they won't build up inside. Keeping difficult emotions inside can make people feel worse.

Kids can talk about their feelings with their parents. They could also talk to a trusted adult such as a teacher or coach. Some children might go to a **counselor**. Friends can be good listeners, too. It might help to talk to a friend who has gone through his or her own parents' divorce. If a person's feelings are too hard to talk about, he or she could try writing in a journal.

Kids may have questions during a divorce. They might wonder who they will live with. They might want to know if they will still go to the same school. Asking questions will help kids know what to expect. This can help people feel less worried.

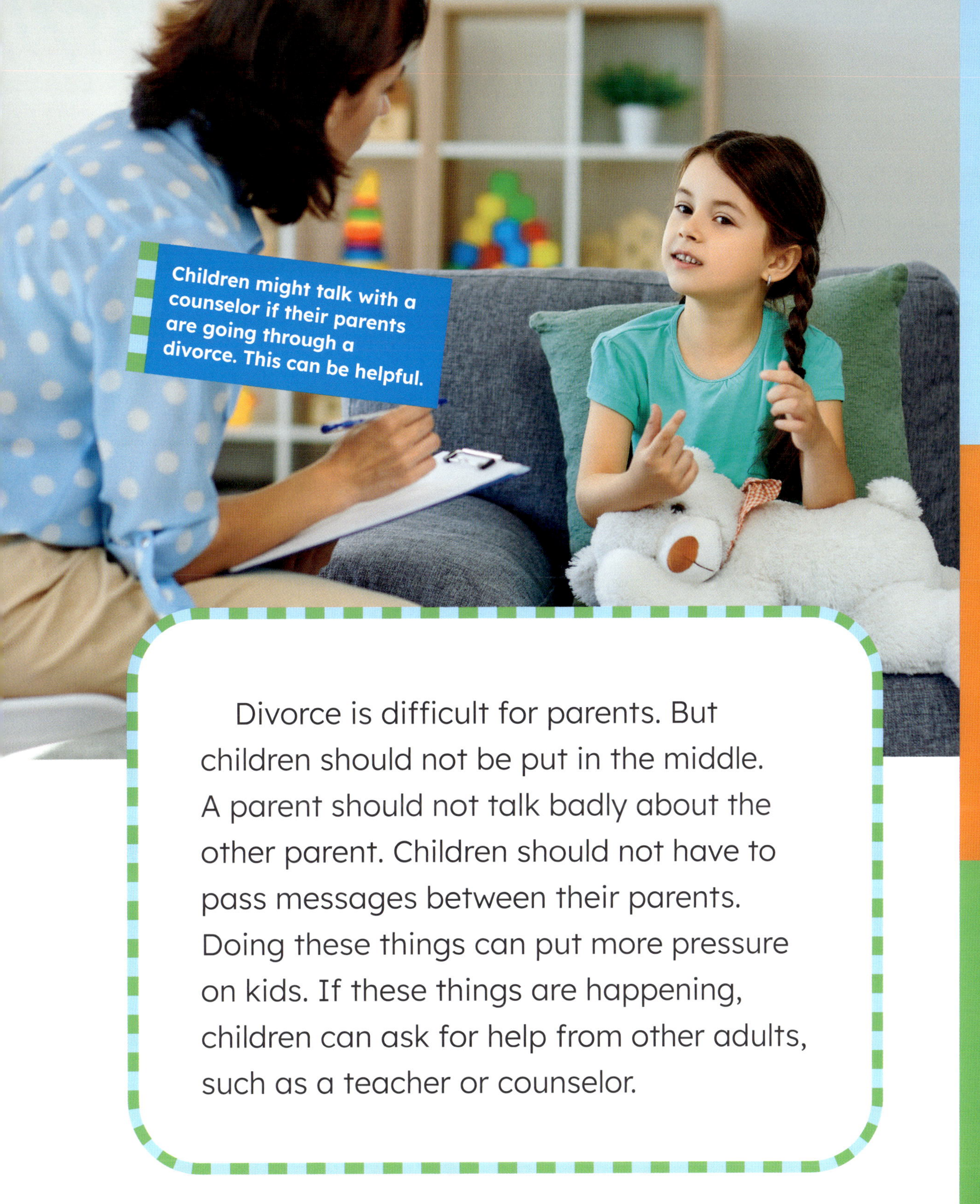

Children might talk with a counselor if their parents are going through a divorce. This can be helpful.

Divorce is difficult for parents. But children should not be put in the middle. A parent should not talk badly about the other parent. Children should not have to pass messages between their parents. Doing these things can put more pressure on kids. If these things are happening, children can ask for help from other adults, such as a teacher or counselor.

Helping a Friend Deal with Divorce

Someone might have a friend whose parents are going through a divorce. It is important to be there for friends when they are going through tough times. A person can ask his or her friends how they are feeling. People might feel more comfortable sharing their feelings when someone else starts the conversation. Regularly asking how a friend is doing shows that a person cares.

People can talk with their friends about how they are feeling. This can help them feel better.

A person doesn't have to solve her friend's problems. Just listening to how the friend feels can help.

Learning to Listen

It is important to be a good listener. To be a good listener, people can face their friend. They can make eye contact and focus on the friend. It is important to not interrupt when a friend is talking. People can also ask questions or repeat what the friend is saying. This shows that they are listening.

A friend may not want to talk about the divorce. That is OK, too. It is important to respect how the person is feeling. Instead of talking, people could invite their friend over for a playdate. This could be a good break from what is going on at home. When a person's friend is ready to talk, he or she should be ready to listen. Being a good listener shows friends that they have someone to talk to.

Sometimes it is hard to know what to say when a friend shares his or her feelings about divorce. Divorce causes many changes in a person's life. People could talk to their friend about how she coped with other big changes. Maybe she got a new sibling or pet. Maybe she started a new school or joined a club. All of these changes caused uncertainty.

Families can still be happy after divorce.

People could talk about how she got through these changes. She might do the same things to deal with divorce.

It is OK to feel difficult emotions during a divorce. Change is not easy. Being upset or anxious is normal. But there are ways to feel better. It is possible to be happy. Things get better over time.

Wonder More

Wondering about New Information

How much did you know about divorce before reading this book? What new information did you learn? Write down three new facts that this book taught you. Was the new information surprising? Why or why not?

Wondering How It Matters

What is one way divorce relates to your life? If you cannot think of a personal connection, imagine a way the topic might affect other kids. What impact might it have on their lives?

Wondering Why

Why do you think it's important to learn about how to deal with divorce? How might learning about this topic help you?

Ways to Keep Wondering

After reading this book, what questions do you have about divorce? What can you do to learn more about how to deal with divorce?

Fast Facts

- A divorce is when two people end their marriage.
- A divorce can change a family. For instance, children might live with one parent or move between two homes.
- Kids might feel anxious, angry, or sad if their parents get a divorce. These feelings are OK.
- It is important for kids to continue taking care of themselves during challenging times. Kids can talk about their feelings, stick to a routine, and ask questions.
- If a friend's parents are going through a divorce, people can be good listeners to help him or her. They can also schedule a playdate to have fun with their friend.
- Friends can be good listeners by focusing on the person speaking, making eye contact, and not interrupting.

Glossary

adapt (uh-DAPT) To adapt means to become used to new situations. It might take time to adapt to a new routine.

anxious (ANGK-shuhs) Anxious means to feel worried or nervous about something uncertain. Many people feel anxious about big changes.

cope (KOPE) To cope means to deal with a challenge. People might cope with divorce by talking to a counselor or writing in a journal.

counselor (KOWN-suh-lur) A counselor is a person who helps people work through strong feelings. A child might talk to a counselor if her parents are getting divorced.

eye contact (EYE KON-takt) Making eye contact means looking another person in the eyes. Eye contact can show that a person is listening.

guilty (GIL-tee) When a person feels guilty, he feels like he did something wrong. Children should not feel guilty if their parents get a divorce.

routines (roo-TEENZ) Routines are sets of things that people do regularly. One of the family's routines was going to bed at 8 p.m. every night.

Find Out More

In the Library

An, Priscilla. *Mindfulness with Family.* Parker, CO: The Child's World, 2024.

Miller, Marie-Therese. *Families Like Mine.* Minneapolis, MN: Lerner, 2021.

Orgullo, Marisa. *What Happens When My Parents Get Divorced?* New York, NY: PowerKids Press, 2018.

On the Web

Visit our website for links about dealing with divorce:
childsworld.com/links

Note to Parents, Caregivers, Teachers, and Librarians: We routinely verify our Web links to make sure they are safe and active sites. So encourage your readers to check them out!

Index